MENUS
for
MEERKATS
and
Other Hungry
Animals

WORDS BY
BEN HOARE

ART BY
HUI SKIPP

First American Edition 2024
Kane Miller, A Division of EDC Publishing

A Raspberry Book
Art direction and cover design: Sidonie Beresford-Browne
Internal design: Vanessa Mee
Editorial: Tracey Turner
Consultant: Ben Hoare
Copyright © Raspberry Books Ltd 2023

For information contact:
Kane Miller, A Division of EDC Publishing
5402 S 122nd E Ave
Tulsa, OK 74146
www.kanemiller.com
www.paperpie.com

Library of Congress Control Number: 2023938377

Printed in China
1 2 3 4 5 6 7 8 9 10

ISBN: 978-1-68464-830-6

Kane Miller
A DIVISION OF EDC PUBLISHING

CONTENTS

HUNGRY ANIMALS

EVERY ANIMAL HAS TO EAT. FOOD IS A SOURCE OF ENERGY, WHICH ALL CREATURES NEED TO KEEP THEIR BODIES WORKING AND DO LOTS OF OTHER ESSENTIAL THINGS. WITHOUT FOOD, THEY CAN'T MOVE, GROW, OR STAY FIT AND HEALTHY. FOOD ALSO GIVES ANIMALS THE STRENGTH TO BREED, GIVE BIRTH, AND LOOK AFTER THEIR YOUNG.

But what is food, exactly?

Food can be just about anything! Animals called herbivores have a vegetarian menu, including grass, leaves, fruits, seeds, flower nectar, and bark. Then there are carnivores, which have other animals on their menu. Animals known as omnivores have a menu that features both plants and meat.

Some animals are VERY fussy and will only eat one thing—for example, koalas eat almost nothing except the leaves of their favorite tree. Other animals like food that you or I might find disgusting—there are even animals that have soil or poop for dinner. Mmmm.

In this book, you will discover hungry creatures from all over the world with very different diets. There are mighty blue whales that gulp colossal mouthfuls of sea creatures, clever meerkats that munch scorpions without getting stung, and many more. They are all wonders of nature.

Come on, let's see what's on the menu … it's dinnertime!

MEERKAT MENU

This menu features a lot of wriggling insects, a few other small creatures, and some plants. Meerkats must be careful: some of their food fights back!

MAIN COURSE

INSECTS
including beetles, termites, crickets, and ants

GRUBS
(which are young insects, also known as larvae)

SOLIFUGES
(or camel spiders)

SCORPIONS

SPIDERS

CENTIPEDES and MILLIPEDES

EGGS

SMALL RODENTS and LIZARDS

PLANTS

including tsamma (a type of watermelon) and gemsbok cucumber

DRINKS

Even though they live in very dry places, there's nothing to drink on the menu because meerkats get all the moisture they need from the juicy animals and plants they eat.

WHERE MEERKATS LIVE

DINNER WITH THE
MEERKATS

LENGTH:
20 INCHES,
including tail
~
WEIGHT:
AROUND 2 POUNDS
Female meerkats are
bigger than males, and are
in charge of the group.

Meerkats live in large groups in the deserts and grasslands of southern Africa. They spend most of their time looking for food and eating it, so dinner lasts all day.

SCORPION STINGS

Adult meerkats have resistance to the venom contained in a scorpion's sting, so they aren't in danger if they do get stung. They carefully remove the scorpion's stinger for the younger members of their meerkat group. Many of the scorpions eaten by meerkats inject venom so powerful that it would be dangerous even for human beings, who are many times bigger than a meerkat.

DIGGING for DINNER

Meerkats have an excellent sense of smell and are very good at sniffing out insects and other small creatures, even if they're hiding underground. Meerkats can dig very quickly with their sharp claws to unearth them.

MEERKATS on the MENU

Meerkats are dinner for other animals. They're preyed on by eagles, hawks, jackals, and snakes. One or more meerkats stands upright on its hind legs on the lookout for predators while the others search for food or look after young meerkats. The lookout makes a high-pitched cry if it spots a predator, which sends the other meerkats running for cover. There are different warning cries depending on which type of predator has been spotted.

DANGEROUS SNACKS

Meerkats deal with other perilous prey, too. Solifuges, sometimes known as camel spiders or sun spiders, are relatives of spiders and scorpions. They are aggressive, fast, and can deliver very nasty bites with their huge, supersharp jaws. Other dangerous prey animals include venomous spiders, and biting, spike-covered armored crickets. Meerkats are usually fast and nimble enough to avoid harm, but eating can be an energetic and risky occupation.

BEETLE CLEANING SERVICE

When they're not looking for food, or on guard duty, meerkats live in underground burrows. They have some surprising housemates: although beetles are the most common prey for meerkats, there's a type of dung beetle that meerkats don't like to eat, which shares the meerkat burrow. The beetles eat the meerkats' dung, so the meerkats get a free cleaning service.

SCARLET MACAW MENU

The scarlet macaw is a parrot with a menu of delicious nuts, fruit, leaves, and flowers. For dessert, it might sip sugary sap, tear some bark off trees, or nibble raw earth.

MAIN COURSE

NUTS

SEEDS

FRUIT

BLOSSOMS

NECTAR

LEAVES

SIDES

SAP
(a golden, gooey liquid inside trees)

TREE BARK

CLAY
(scraped from cliffs and riverbanks)

WHERE SCARLET MACAWS LIVE

DRINKS

Macaws get plenty of water from the juicy fruit they eat, but still need to drink daily. They don't have to fly far to find a refreshing stream, river, or pool in the rain forest.

DINNER WITH THE
SCARLET MACAWS

Shortly after daybreak, macaws screech through the rain forest to begin looking for food. The rainbow-colored parrots will fly 10 miles or more to find fresh supplies, and scan the tops of trees as they go. Every day is one long meal!

CRACKING POWER

Scarlet macaws have superstrong bills for cracking nuts. They eat the nuts of many different trees, and can crack much bigger and harder nuts than other animals. Some of the nuts have thick shells as tough as a coconut! The bill's hooked tip is also great for ripping leaves and bark off trees.

DELICATE TOUCH

Though the macaws have powerful bills, they can be delicate feeders, too. They use their fat, muscular tongue to roll seeds around their mouth. This way, they are able to strip off the inedible husk to get at the tasty part inside. Macaws also love nibbling colorful tree blossoms. They sip the sugary nectar in flowers and lick the sticky sap that dribbles down tree trunks.

LENGTH: 32–36 INCHES,
half of which is tail
~
WEIGHT: 2–3 POUNDS

HEALTHY CLAY

Every day, large flocks of macaws gather at steep cliffs, often on riverbanks in the forest. They come to eat the red or yellow clay, which they scrape off and swallow. This might sound strange, but for the macaws, it is essential. Minerals in the clay most likely help to wipe out the nasty toxins in their diet, which come from eating unripe seeds and fruit.

FOREST ACROBATS

Macaws are excellent acrobats, which helps when feeding high above the forest floor. It's just as well because some rain forest trees, such as the kapok, may be as tall as a 20-story building! Their amazingly long tail gives them balance, and their strong toes grip branches firmly. A macaw can perch on one foot, while using the other to hold food.

INTELLIGENT BIRDS

Scarlet macaws stay with the same partner year after year and may live for up to 50 years in the wild. During their long life together, each pair of birds builds up a detailed knowledge of their rain forest home, which makes it easier to locate food. When they meet other macaws, they share news about the best feeding places, so everyone benefits.

GRIZZLY BEAR MENU

Many things are on the menu for a grizzly bear—plants, insects, and other animals all taste good to a grizzly. They need to eat a lot to keep them going in winter.

MAIN COURSE

NUTS
including hazelnuts

BERRIES
blueberries, grouse whortleberries, elderberries, and lots more

ROOTS
such as sweet cicely, biscuit root, and peavine roots

MANY OTHER PLANTS
including dandelions, clover, and lots more

SIDES

GRUBS
(which are young insects, or larvae)

INSECTS
including ants, bees, wasps, and moths

EARTHWORMS

LARGER ANIMALS
(including dead ones), such as …

GOPHERS   CARIBOU   MOOSE

GROUND SQUIRRELS   ELK and **BISON**   FISH (especially salmon)

(usually young ones)

DRINKS

Grizzlies drink water from rivers, lakes, and estuaries (which contain salt water as well as fresh water).

DINNER WITH THE
GRIZZLY BEARS

Grizzlies in Canada and Alaska grow bigger than those that live farther south because they eat more fish.

Grizzly bears are a type of North American brown bear that get their name because they sometimes have white-tipped, or "grizzled," fur. There's not much on the menu in winter, but the rest of the year is one long feast.

FLEXITARIAN BEARS

Grizzly bears are big, powerful animals with long, sharp claws. But they mostly use their claws for digging dens and finding plants to eat, rather than pouncing on other animals. As omnivores, plants make up around three-quarters of their diet. They dig up roots, and munch on berries, grasses, leaves, stems, and flowers. Dandelion flowers are a favorite.

FEASTS and FASTS

From spring until autumn, grizzlies eat almost **ALL** the time. They need to store up fat for winter, which they spend in their dens, sleeping a lot, and not eating or drinking at all. Female grizzlies need extra energy because they give birth to their cubs in the den during the winter. By springtime, grizzlies emerge from their dens, very hungry.

MEATY TREATS

Grizzly bears eat more meat in spring than at other times of year. They can sniff out a dead animal's body from 15 miles away, and they often feed on bison and other animals that have died over the winter. The bears also hunt animals as big as moose and elk, as well as squirrels and gophers, using their long claws to dig up gopher burrows.

MINIBEAST MEALS

Insects and earthworms are also tasty to grizzlies. In the western United States, miller moths are common, and one grizzly bear can eat 40,000 of them a day! Bears also eat wasps, ants, termites, and bees. They pull apart beehives, but are more interested in the bees and larvae inside than in the honey.

FISHING BEARS

Salmon swim from the ocean to lay their eggs in rivers in autumn, fighting against the current and leaping up waterfalls. Grizzly bears that live near salmon rivers become skilled at fishing. If there are lots of salmon to eat, the bears often eat only the fattiest bits, like the head and the eggs, and throw the rest away.

GREAT WHITE SHARK MENU

The menu for these sharks includes seals, dolphins, sea lions, and fish, as well as meat from dead whales. Great white sharks will eat birds and turtles too.

MAIN COURSE

SEA LIONS

TUNA

DOLPHINS
(especially baby dolphins, called calves)

SEALS

BODIES of DEAD WHALES

OTHER SHARKS

SIDES

SEA TURTLES

PENGUINS

DRINKS

Sharks don't drink, but they take in salty seawater through their gills, which look like five slits on each side of their body. They have a special system for getting rid of the salt.

WHERE GREAT WHITE SHARKS LIVE

In oceans throughout the world, except for in the far north and far south.

DINNER WITH THE
GREAT WHITE SHARKS

Fast and powerful with a crunching bite, great white sharks are top ocean predators. They cruise long distances to find prey and can go two months between meals, but prefer to fill up on meat every 12–15 days.

KILLING POWER

Great white sharks have 300 triangular teeth up to 2.75 inches long, with jagged cutting edges like the teeth of a saw. Though their jaws are huge, they cannot chew. They shake their heads from side to side to tear off great chunks of flesh, which they swallow whole. Very occasionally, they mistake a swimmer or surfer for their normal prey, but such attacks are incredibly rare. Each year, only around 10 people die from shark bites worldwide.

CHANGING DIET

Like all sharks, great whites are born predators, so their very first meal will be meat. When still young, they catch a variety of small prey, which might include fish, turtles, and seabirds, such as penguins. Over the years, as they become larger, their appetite grows. Adult sharks like to hunt large mammals with plenty of blubber on their body, especially seals, sea lions, and dolphins.

WHALE MEAT

When a whale dies, its massive body fills with gas and floats at the surface. It's now an easy meal for sharks, which don't mind feeding on smelly, rotting flesh. Great white sharks usually live on their own, but when there is a meal as big as this, several of them will often turn up and share the feast.

SURPRISE ATTACK

As a great white shark homes in on prey, it accelerates to as much as 30 mph. It attacks from below, surging upward toward its target like a missile, sometimes bursting right out of the water. These sharks are intelligent hunters. They know that young animals are slow and inexperienced, so they patrol the coasts where seal and sea lion mothers have their babies.

SUPER SENSES

Great whites can hear things moving up to a mile away, and smell prey from hundreds of yards. They are able to taste minuscule amounts of blood in the water, and by following this scent trail, home in on injured or dying animals. As they get closer, they start to feel vibrations in the water and can even detect the tiny electric signals produced by an animal's muscles.

KOALA MENU

Koalas are incredibly fussy eaters. Their menu features a lot of leaves, which koalas prefer to pick from only a few kinds of eucalyptus tree.

MAIN COURSE

LEAVES of EUCALYPTUS TREES
(also called gum trees) including ...

Blue gum

River red gum

Manna gum

Grey gum

SIDES

For a change, koalas sometimes munch leaves from several other trees, including wattle trees and tea trees.

WATTLE TREE LEAVES

TEA TREE LEAVES

GRAVEL and EARTH

(because it helps them digest all those leaves!)

DRINKS

Most of the water koalas need comes from their leafy diet. But when it rains, they can't resist licking the wet bark of tree trunks.

WHERE KOALAS LIVE

DINNER WITH THE

KOALAS

Koalas live in Australia in eucalyptus forests. Their leafy dinner lasts around four hours, usually at night, and then they doze off. They eat so many eucalyptus leaves, they end up smelling of them!

HOLDING TIGHT

To reach their favorite leaves, koalas have become expert tree climbers. Their arms and legs are strong, with sharp claws for extra grip, and the toes on their front paws curl together like pincers to grab branches. Most of their life is spent high above the ground, but from time to time, they come down to move to a new feeding tree.

LEAF MUNCHERS

There are more than 700 kinds of eucalyptus tree in Australia, though koalas feed on only 20–30 of them. The eucalyptus leaves must be fresh, so they sniff out tasty ones and ignore the rest. Each dinnertime, koalas eat 10–15 ounces of leaves. But since the leaves are tough and stringy, three-quarters of what they eat passes straight through them, and they get rid of it in their poop.

REST and DIGEST

Eucalyptus leaves are low in protein and other nutrients, and don't contain much energy. So koalas don't do anything fast, and look like they're moving in slow motion. They spend much of their day just sitting in trees, chewing leaves ready for swallowing, and sleeping for 20 hours out of every 24! They love to squeeze into a cozy space between a branch and the tree trunk to nod off.

BABY DIET

Though koalas may remind you of teddy bears, they are not bears at all. They belong to a group of mammals called marsupials, which also includes kangaroos and wombats. The baby koala lives in a pouch on its mother's belly and later moves onto her back, clinging on like a living backpack. It drinks her milk for six months, and also guzzles her droppings! This might sound odd, but the droppings contain a bacteria the youngster will need to be able to feed on eucalyptus.

POISONOUS LEAVES

Eucalyptus leaves are full of poisons, or toxins, and koalas are virtually the only animals that can eat them without getting ill. They have a special organ called a caecum, which houses millions of tiny bacteria. The bacteria break down the toxins in their food to make it safe.

DUNG BEETLE MENU

All over the world except for Antarctica.

Dung beetles make a meal from the waste other animals leave behind. For the wriggly young beetle grubs, there is only poop on the menu. Many adult beetles don't eat anything at all, but gather dung for the grubs.

CHILDREN'S MENU

ELEPHANT DUNG
(massive mounds weighing several pounds each)

HORSE DUNG
(soft dollops full of grass stems)

ADULT MENU

Some adult beetles sip the liquid inside dung, and some feed on dung, fungi, plants, and animals.

DRINKS

Dung beetle grubs never get thirsty because their stinky food is nice and wet. Delicious!

ANTELOPE DUNG
(grape-sized poop balls)

CATTLE DUNG
(cow pies: smooth, juicy poop pancakes)

RABBIT DROPPINGS
(little poop pellets)

DINNER WITH THE
DUNG BEETLES

Dung beetles are found all over the world, wherever there's plenty of dung. Believe it or not, their dinner is so tasty to them that they will fight to get their share. The grubs, called larvae, munch through it for several weeks, then turn into adult beetles.

FINDING DUNG

Adult dung beetles have an amazing sense of smell and can sniff out fresh dung from hundreds of yards away. They quickly fly or march toward the smelly treat. Sometimes, the first beetles arrive within minutes of the dung being dumped! A large heap of elephant, rhino, or buffalo dung may attract hundreds of shiny beetles.

DEALING with DUNG

Some beetles dig straight into the dung, lay their eggs in it, and their grubs hatch a few days later surrounded by their favorite food. Some dig a tunnel under the dung for their eggs. Others break off a chunk of dung and shape it into a ball, then roll it away over the ground to a safe spot, where they bury it. When the grubs hatch, their underground chamber is stuffed with a supply of dung.

FULL of GOODNESS

Most dung beetles live in grasslands, fields, and plains, which are home to large herds of grazing animals, known as herbivores. Herbivores only half digest their food before dropping the remains as dung, and that means it still contains lots of nutrients for the beetle grubs to enjoy.

LENGTH: UP TO 6.5 INCHES

~

WEIGHT: UP TO 3.5 OUNCES

(Most dung beetles are smaller than this though!)

SUPER STRENGTH

To help them push their poop balls, dung beetles have strong legs with a superb grip. One large species is able to heave a ball over 1,100 times its own body weight. That's like a 150-pound adult human lifting six full double-decker buses! Amazingly, the beetles push the dung balls in a perfectly straight line, even though they do it backward and can't see where they are going. They find their way using light from the Sun, Moon, and stars.

CLEANUP CREW

Dung beetles do an extremely useful job: without their hard work, vast amounts of dung would start to pile up everywhere. By clearing it away, they return its nutrients to the soil. And the dung often has seeds in it, which the beetles help to spread far and wide. Long ago, the Ancient Egyptians worshipped dung beetles and believed that they rolled the Sun across the sky each day.

ORANGUTAN MENU

This forest menu includes all sorts of tasty food, including fruit, flowers, leaves, and bark from over 400 types of trees and plants. Honey, eggs, and small animals are eaten by these shaggy red apes, too.

MAIN COURSE

FLOWERS

WILD HONEY

TREE BARK

RIPE FRUIT
including figs (the favorite!), durian, rough laurel, and wild rambutan

LEAVES and SHOOTS

durian

rough laurel

wild rambutan

figs

SIDES

TREE FROGS, LIZARDS, and BIRDS

(though it's very rare for orangutans to catch and eat these animals)

BIRDS' EGGS

INSECTS

including termites, ants, bees, crickets, and caterpillars

DRINKS

Orangutans poke their furry fingers into tree holes full of water, then hold them up so water dribbles into their mouth. After a rain shower, they might also drink from wet leaves or their shaggy fur!

WHERE ORANGUTANS LIVE

31

DINNER WITH THE

ORANGUTANS

HEAD and BODY LENGTH: 4 TO 4.7 FEET

WEIGHT: UP TO 175 POUNDS

An adult male is twice as heavy as an adult female.

Orangutans are the world's biggest tree-living animals. Every day they spend hours traveling through the rain forests of Southeast Asia in search of dinner, eating as they go. Their first choice is fresh fruit, though, and they make a special effort to find it.

FABULOUS FRUIT

Fruit makes up two-thirds of the orangutan menu. There is one fruit that orangutans adore above all others—the fig. When they come across a tree full of figs, they stay to gorge on as many as they can. Orangutans also like durian fruit, which some people say stinks of sweaty socks and rotting fish! They peel the spiny skin and feast on the smelly flesh.

ACROBATIC APES

If they can find it, orangutans will eat several pounds of fruit a day. To help them climb and pick fruit, they have extremely long, strong arms and can grip branches with their hands and their feet. They eat, drink, wash, and sleep high up in trees—unlike chimps and gorillas, they hardly ever come to the ground.

USING TOOLS

As a treat, orangutans love the sweet honey made by forest bees. Getting this food is tricky, and some orangutans use a tool to help them. They choose a sharp stick and chew one end so it frays, like the end of a mop. Then they hold it in their mouth and poke the frayed end into the nest to scoop out the honey. They use the same clever trick to fish termites (ant-like insects) out of their nest.

FOREST GARDENERS

When orangutans move around the rain forest, they are actually doing their bit to help the forest grow by planting seeds wherever they go. This is because the fruit they eat is full of seeds, which they spread in their poop. The seeds come to no harm inside their stomach and gut, and pass out in perfect condition, ready to sprout. Even better, the poop acts as a dollop of fertilizer for the baby tree or plant!

LEARNING from MOTHER

Knowing where to find food in the rain forest takes many years. Youngsters watch their mother feed to work out what tastes good and what to avoid. They see how she always selects ripe fruit and the youngest, juiciest leaves, and how she carefully peels the bark off branches to reach the soft part underneath.

INDIAN COBRA MENU

On the menu for the Indian cobra are small animals like rats, mice, squirrels, lizards, and birds. This big snake has powerful venom to stop them in their tracks, so they need to watch out.

MAIN COURSE

SMALL BIRDS
(which are often caught while roosting at night)

MICE

SQUIRRELS
such as Indian palm squirrels

RATS
including rice rats

LIZARDS
including oriental garden lizards

SIDES

FROGS
including skipper frogs and tree frogs

BIRDS' EGGS

WHERE INDIAN COBRAS LIVE

DRINKS

Cobras can't suck or sip like we do. To drink, they dip their head into a puddle or pool and open their mouth, so that water soaks into the skin of their lower jaw.

DINNER WITH THE
INDIAN COBRAS

These snakes live in southern Asia and go hunting by day or night.
Their eyesight is poor, but they are amazingly good at sniffing out prey.
After dinner, they may not eat anything else for several weeks or even months.

ON the HUNT

The Indian cobra's top targets are small mammals, such as rats and mice. It finds plenty of them in farmers' fields and around villages and towns, and slides into buildings to search there! If it meets anything it sees as a threat, it stretches its head and neck into a hood to make itself look bigger and more frightening.

DEADLY VENOM

Cobra venom is a kind of toxin, or poison, and comes from large glands behind each eye. It flows out through a pair of incredibly sharp teeth called fangs in the snake's upper jaw. When the cobra strikes, the fangs stab the venom into the prey. It paralyzes muscles so the victim is unable to move, and can even kill an animal straightaway. Indian cobras sometimes kill people, too.

OPEN WIDE

Like all snakes, the Indian cobra lacks chewing teeth—it must swallow food whole. If its prey was struggling, this would be difficult! Luckily, its venom makes victims easy to swallow. Its jaws are super flexible and open far enough to fit prey wider than itself. Strong throat muscles then push the meal down to the cobra's stomach. You can actually see a bulge move along the snake.

A DANGEROUS ENEMY

Few predators dare to tackle snakes as venomous as Indian cobras. Even newly hatched baby cobras, which are less than 8 inches long, have venom in their bite! However, Indian cobras are on the menu of one other animal. The king cobra is even larger than they are, and its favorite dinner is … SNAKES.

DIGESTING FOOD

Swallowing meals whole might give *you* a stomachache, but the Indian cobra simply hides away and rests for a while to digest its food. The powerful acids in its stomach can break down most things, including bones. But they can't deal with fur, feathers, or lizard scales, so the cobra gets rid of those in its poop.

BLUE WHALE MENU

This menu features one main food. As it cruises the ocean, the giant blue whale slurps mighty mouthfuls of it. The animals it eats are tiny, so it eats vast amounts of them!

MAIN COURSE

KRILL ...

... KRILL ...

... and MORE KRILL

(up to 40 million of them a day)! Krill are shrimplike animals up to 2.3 inches long.

SIDES

OTHER TINY ANIMALS, including ...

COPEPODS

AMPHIPODS

SEA ANGELS
(a shell-less snail)

FISH and SQUID

A whale might swallow some fish and squid by accident!

DRINKS

The blue whale doesn't get thirsty because the water it needs comes from its food. When it gulps a meal, almost all the seawater that pours in flows out again.

WHERE BLUE WHALES LIVE

In most oceans around the world except in the very far north.

DINNER WITH THE
BLUE WHALES

LENGTH:
UP TO 100 FEET
~
WEIGHT:
UP TO
200 TONS
Female whales are larger
than males.

Blue whales are the largest animals that have ever lived. They could easily swallow a bus, and can eat around four tons of food a day. Dinnertime lasts a few months, then they eat nothing at all for the rest of the year.

BIG EATER

To satisfy its massive appetite, the blue whale must find a lot of krill, its favorite food. But that is not a problem because krill live in enormous swarms that are so thick, they can turn the surface of the sea red. The whale just swims into a swarm and opens wide.

FILTER FEEDING

The whale's lower jaw has many long folds similar to those in curtains. These stretch as the jaw hinges open to form a huge scoop. Water rushes in and the whale filters out the tasty krill. Finally, it uses its gigantic, elephant-sized tongue to push the waste water out through the sides of its closed mouth.

BRILLIANT BALEEN

Instead of teeth, the whale has something amazing called baleen. Baleen is made of keratin, like human fingernails and hair. It hangs down from the roof of the whale's mouth in great sheets, about 3 feet long. The baleen traps all the krill in each mouthful of seawater, ready for the whale to swallow. It works a bit like a kitchen sieve, but it's much, much bigger!

SUMMER FEAST

The krill that blue whales eat are found in the Arctic Ocean and the Antarctic (Southern) Ocean. Every summer, the whales spend three months in these icy oceans, feeding nonstop. Having put on masses of weight, they swim thousands of miles toward tropical seas. Their next dinner will be the year after, when they return to the cold seas. Until then, they live off their thick layer of blubber.

LIFE-GIVING POOP

Krill are full of nutrients, especially nitrogen and iron—and that means blue whale poop is too. A single whale poop might be 50 gallons, which would fill a bathtub! It is fertilizer for millions of tiny floating plants, which in turn are meals for larger animals. So with every colossal poop, a blue whale helps maintain life in the ocean.

LION MENU

Lions have a meaty menu that includes prey as large as buffalo and giraffes, as well as a selection of smaller animals. Catching their food takes teamwork and great skill.

MAIN COURSE
LARGE ANIMALS including ...

GIRAFFE

IMPALA
(a type of antelope)

PLAINS ZEBRA

AFRICAN BUFFALO

WILDEBEEST
(another antelope)

WARTHOG
(member of the wild pig family)

EMERGENCY SNACK

If they're really hungry, lions may eat ostrich eggs, tortoises, or fish.

SIDES

OSTRICH
(especially young ones) and other large birds

AFRICAN HARE

CRESTED PORCUPINE

DRINKS

Lions live in hot places, including dry and dusty plains, so can go up to four days without water. But they much prefer to drink at a river or water hole every day.

DINNER WITH THE LIONS

MALE:
UP TO 6.5 FEET LONG
AND 420 POUNDS

MALE:
UP TO 6.5 FEET LONG
AND 420 POUNDS

FEMALE: NEARLY
6 FEET LONG AND
285 POUNDS

Lions are one of the top predators in Africa's grasslands and desertlike plains. They live in groups called prides, which hunt together and share the meat afterward. But they only spend a few hours a day hunting, so most of the time they rest.

BUILT to KILL

Lions have extremely powerful jaws and long canine teeth as sharp as carving knives, which means they can kill big animals. They grab prey and break its neck with a crunching bite, or else they bite the throat and squeeze tight. Much of their hunting is done after sunset, thanks to their superb night vision.

TEAMWORK

Prides of lions often include several female lionesses and their cubs, plus one or two big adult males with their magnificent manes. The lionesses are lightest and fastest, so are the best hunters. They team up to chase buffalo, antelope, or zebras to separate the weaker young from the rest of the herd. A few hide among long grass or bushes, while the others chase prey toward their hiding place. At the last moment, the waiting lionesses burst from cover to make the kill.

CATNAP

Male lions need around 6 pounds of food daily, and lionesses just over half that. They can guzzle down a huge amount of meat in one sitting, but then must rest and digest it all. In fact, lions are incredibly sleepy animals—the pride will find a nice, shady spot and doze for up to 21 hours a day!

VARIED DIET

In different parts of Africa, lions feed on different things. And some prides may target a particular kind of prey—for example, there are prides that specialize in hunting wildebeest, and others that hunt giraffes. Lions never miss an opportunity for a meal. On rare occasions, they have even been known to kill young elephants and crocodiles!

STEALING FOOD

Lions can be sneaky, too. If they see cheetahs or hyenas make a kill, or smell a dead body in the distance, they race over to snatch it for themselves. Since lions are heavier and stronger than cheetahs or hyenas, these smaller predators usually give up their food and retreat. Some prides of lions steal as much as half their food.

GLOSSARY

ape a mammal with a big brain, nimble hands, and no tail, such as an orangutan or chimpanzee.

bacteria tiny, single-celled living things that exist in vast numbers in soil, water, air, and the bodies of other living things, including humans.

baleen sieve-like bristles within a whale's mouth.

blubber thick layer of fat under the skin of some sea animals, including whales, dolphins, seals, and sea lions.

canine tooth long front tooth in some meat-eating animals, with a sharp tip for cutting or stabbing flesh. There is one pair in the upper jaw and one pair in the lower jaw.

carnivore an animal that feeds on the flesh of other animals.

clay soft, loose soil or earth that may be eaten by some animals to help their digestion.

fertilizer something that contains nutrients that help plants grow.

gills organs used for breathing underwater, found in fish and some amphibians.

herbivore an animal that eats only plant food, for example, grass or leaves.

herd group of mammals that sticks together for safety, often in open habitats, such as grasslands or deserts.

husk the hard, dry outer covering of a nut or seed, which usually can't be eaten.

larvae insects at the stage of development between the egg and adult stages.

mammal animal that has warm blood and feeds its babies on milk. Most mammals have fur or hair, but this has almost disappeared on sea mammals, such as whales.

mane a patch of long hair or fur around the head or neck of some mammals, such as horses and male lions.

marsupial a type of mammal that gives birth to tiny babies that then grow in a pouch on the mother's belly. Most marsupials, including koalas, kangaroos, and wombats, live in Australia.

nectar a sweet liquid made by flowers, which bees use as fuel and to feed their larvae.

nutrients substances that animals and plants need to stay alive and grow.

omnivore an animal that has a varied diet including both meat and plant foods.

paralyze stop an animal from moving all or part of its body.

poison harmful substance made by an animal as a defense, and which can sometimes cause death. For it to take effect, an animal has to touch or eat the poison.

predator an animal that eats other animals, which are the predator's prey.

prey an animal killed and eaten by other animals, which are known as predators.

rain forest very wet forest where it rains a lot. Most are in tropical parts of the world.

sap a sugary liquid found in plants that carries food to the different parts of the plant.

species a particular kind of living thing. When members of the same species breed together, they produce young. However, members of different species can not breed with each other.

squid a soft-bodied sea creature related to octopuses, with a sharp beak, large eyes, and long tentacles.

termite a small, ant-like insect that lives in large groups called colonies, ruled by a queen.

venom harmful substance made by an animal, which can sometimes cause death. For it to take effect, the venom must be delivered by teeth, claws, or stingers into another animal's body.

INDEX